Split Testing

B. Vincent

Published by RWG Publishing, 2021.

SPLIT TESTING

First edition. August 13, 2021.

Written by B. Vincent.

Also by B. Vincent

Affiliate Marketing
Affiliate Marketing
Affiliate Marketing

Standalone
Business Employee Discipline
Affiliate Recruiting
Business Layoffs & Firings
Business and Entrepreneur Guide
Business Remote Workforce
Career Transition
Project Management
Precision Targeting
Professional Development
Strategic Planning
Content Marketing
Imminent List Building
Getting Past GateKeepers
Banner Ads

Bookkeeping
Bridge Pages
Business Acquisition
Business Bogging
Marketing Automation
Better Meetings
Conversion Optimization
Creative Solutions
Employee Recruitment
Startup Capital
Employee Mentoring
Followership
Servant Leadership
Human Resources
Team Building
Freelancing
Funnel Building
Geo Targeting
Goal Setting
Immanent List Building
Lead Generation
Leadership Course
Leadership Transition
LinkedIn Ads
LinkedIn Marketing
Messenger Marketing
New Management
Newsfeed Ads
Search Ads
Online Learning
Sales Webinars

Side Hustles
Split Testing
Twitter Timeline Advertising

Table of Contents

Split Testing

Welcome to this workshop on split testing in this course, we will cover how to help the display of your pages and offers using split testing. This course is divided into three modules, module one covers typical parts that can be attempted. Module two covers making test assortments and module three covers taking apart the results when this course is done. You'll understand how to effectively smooth out your pages and get higher changes for your business. So, moving right along, we should hop into the essential module. Okay, people, welcome to module one. In this module, our lord will show you typical parts that can be attempted. So, get ready to take a couple of notes and we should bounce straightforwardly in.

Module One

Good. So, we will utilize this point of arrival for instance, and take a gander at the different components that can be parted tried when you're attempting to improve your transformation rates. Presently, something significant that I need to accentuate, and we'll return to it and I'll remind you later is that you can just test one thing for each factor, that you're trying. So, in case you're, in case you're trying two varieties, just a single component ought to be changed between the two. Else you're not going to realize what caused the expanded change. Alright. On the off chance that you begin changing numerous varieties, in the event that you change a feature and a catch and a picture in both of the varieties, all things considered, then, at that point you will not know whether it was the feature or the picture or the duplicate or the foundation or the catch that had the effect. So, it's unimaginably significant that when you are parted trying among two varieties, you're just doing each component in turn so you can totally make certain about.

What has, what sort of impact on your change rates? So how about we simply take it from the top. OK. The feature, the feature is the primary thing that you might actually test in a split test to check whether you improve transformation rate. OK. What's more, essentially on the off chance that you have an exceptional selling recommendation or numerous points that could be alluring about your item, you would need to sort out some way to consolidate them in which ones to underscore, in light of the fact that there's just so many words you can squeezed into a feature, correct? That is to say, that is the general purpose of the feature is that it's quite quick and painless. You need to stand out enough to be noticed, correct? Furthermore, you can indeed remember a limited amount a lot of data for there. So exceptionally similarly as an irregular model, how about we take things to a more significant level. Sounds sort of cool, but on the other hand it's actual obscure, correct? Imagine a scenario where the feature was somewhat beefier and said, let me tell you the best way to help your income by 30%, that is more explicit, and it may perform better.

We don't realize we would need to test it. My conjecture is it presumably would, however that is the place of a split test. So, what we need to do is make one page with this feature, which we as of now have. Furthermore, another page with that other feature and leave any remaining components the equivalent. They need to stay consistent between those two-page varieties. Presently, the following thing you can change is symbolism. Symbolism is really incredible on greeting pages, and it can have the effect among high and low change rates. So, a ton of things to consider are your intended interest group. You need to ensure that any human characters in your pictures we'll be relatable or have the ideal impact on your crowd. So, if your crowd, is definitely not a specific segment bunch, just to give you a model, on the off chance that you begin seeing, and this is a genuine model here, if you somehow happened to begin seeing dependent on your email communication with individuals in your client local area, that a significant number of them are old.

A large number of them are retired people are coming up on retirement. Indeed, learn to expect the unexpected. You ought to likely have some silver hair in your pictures. So that it's relatable, correct? Sexual orientation is enormous. There's contending concentrates out there with respect to whether a female is bound to purchase something. In the event that she sees a male or an individual female, and clearly relies upon what sort of item you're selling, same thing with a man. Is it true that he is bound to purchase something? On the off chance that he sees a female or a male? It depends. In case you're selling, you know, manly items, you know, something like a major masculine, you know, antiperspirant brand on the, you presumably need to see men on screen utilizing it clearly, however would you be able to consolidate sex into it? For instance, women who are intrigued by the smell of the antiperspirant, isn't that so? There's a science behind the entirety of this, however what you can do is somewhat skirt the science and just split test with the distinctions.

So, we could in a real sense have a picture like this and afterward have precisely the same picture or practically the same, same posture or comparative posture in any event, however, have a female here, split, test them, and see what the distinctions. Furthermore, in the event that you see a critical distinction for sure, go with it, go with the champ. Alright. Something else to consider about symbolism is substantial, seen esteem, contingent upon your intended interest group. It might get you further to have a bunch of a lot of what were plainly, you know, imagine advanced models of computerized items, alright? Since in certain individuals that kind of enacts this sensation of, amazing, that is a thing. Also, I need to get my hands on it. I need to have that, right. However, you could likewise test this with simply a theoretical picture of an individual with a feature close to them, or an individual grinning, or a, you know, a business visionary remaining in their business environment or something to that effect.

No computerized items being addressed at all and check whether that works better indeed, ensure that is the solitary component that you're trying and afterward see what the victor is straightaway. There's the duplicate, which is the real content. The expressions of your message. This is vital. Notwithstanding, it's not exactly as simple to simply, you know, play trick with this is on the grounds that there's a great deal of it. There's different words, various sentences, correct? Thus, most likely in case you will part test distinctive duplicate, they will be totally unique. Alright. You will change which point is accentuated relying upon what you're selling or offering free of charge. There's likely various advertising points that you could push that may be applicable to various objective business sectors. Thus, you could have point one and point two and see which one works best. So, for instance, in this duplicate, you'll see, there's kind of a supposition that a business exists.

This driving force course will take your business to a higher level. This is what it incorporates yet imagine a scenario where we split tried that against identical page, yet the duplicate was unique, and the point was somewhat unique. What's more, in this next variety, what was really being underscored was an individual who doesn't have a current, effective financial specialist who has been battling. So, at last once, and for all quit battling and we'll get your business going or something to that effect. Also, test those two distinctive showcasing points of duplicate against one another and see which one resounds the most with your traffic. And afterward at long last, there's the catch. Presently, this is somewhat of a questionable region in light of the fact that there's kin who swear that changing the shade of a catch can colossally affect transformation rates. And afterward there's kin who feel that that is simply senseless.

So, the right answer is most likely some place in the center. There is proof that various tones bring about various conduct or diverse mental consequences for watchers. Red ordinarily means earnestness, and yet, red can likewise mean no blue normally means trust simultaneously. Blue could hypothetically not get your kin invigorated enough for adequately excited. And afterward there's marking if brand tones and subject tones, you know, that are essential for your personality are imperative to you and keeping an alluring page are critical to you. Then, at that point you probably won't have as numerous choices to definitely change to only one explicit shading on your purchase button. However, in the event that you do have the adaptability to run a fast test among blue and red, something straightforward like that, just to see if it has an effect. Indeed, it very well may merit doing as such.

Furthermore, assuming the hole among them is adequately huge, Bravo, you have a victor. You can go with whatever shading that was essentially for that specific presentation page. Lastly, it's not simply the shade of the catch. It's likewise so the duplicate of the catch. Alright. So, the diverse phrasing take it to a more elevated level is somewhat of a cool sounding expression, smidgen more unclear, isn't that so? Get the course could be something that you test against that one region on which there's been a ton of study is the perspective of the content. So, in case it's composed according to the perspective of the peruser and the peruser sees the catch, that is saying, give me the free report versus download your free report. There's been a few examinations and tests in the past that have shown that the, give me the free report. Which means talking according to the point of view of the peruser has a higher change rate. It's presumably not continually going to be the situation, but since that marvel exists out there, it very well may be a keen thing to test on your pages. So those are a few instances of things that you could part test. Keep in mind, consistently remember between two varieties, just have one component unique. In any case there's no reason for testing. Okay. And afterward the normal components that we discussed were feature symbolism, duplicate, and fastens.

Module Two

Hello people, welcome to module two. In this module, our master will tell you the best way to make test varieties. So, prepare to take a few notes and we should directly bounce in.

Good. So, this will be a beautiful speedy stroll through of the real specialized part of making a split test. Presently, contingent upon what sort of deals page or lead page programming you're working with, the interaction and the UI may be somewhat unique, however the overall standards are something very similar and most top of the line virtual products do have this AB split testing usefulness. So, you may very well need to borrow a smidgen or reach out to the help group for your product. Also, you'll have the option to do exactly the same thing paying little mind to what you're utilizing for our situation, we're utilizing Insta page, which is an incredibly, acceptable greeting page programming. Furthermore, here's the page we were taking a gander at prior in the past exercise. So, after some time pondering the best thing to change on this page, suppose we concluded that the main thing we need to test is the feature. OK. We're taking a gander at everything. Everything appears to be very acceptable, yet that feature appears to be somewhat obscure. OK. So, we should feel free to click make an AB test up here in the upper left this here. Just became variety a when we did that. So presently we will make another variety.

This is variety B. They appear to be identical. We should feel free to change the duplicate of the feature. How about we feel free to change this a smidgen. In the event that we can get it to fit on one line. Good. So presently we have what is basically a more explicit feature instead of simply take things to a higher level or to a more elevated level. Presently we're really mentioning to the possibility what the advantages of this driving force will be transformations and deals and individuals can right away sort out precisely what the focal point of this genius will be. So, there's almost certain that that will most likely perform significantly better. If we somehow happened to hit update, that would be distributed as a variety. Presently, the manner in which this works is that starting now and into the foreseeable future, there will be a 50, 50 split, an equivalent split. So, when you're sending traffic to this page from this second forward, the first next individual will go to variety B, the following individual will go to variety.

And it will substitute separating left, right left, right left, isn't that so? Stomach muscle AB, so you have half in the two pools, and you can see similarly what the exhibition level of each separate one is currently, contingent upon what sort of programming you're utilizing. It is feasible to run a multi-variate split test where you can come on here, hit new variety. We have another here and we can change the feature once more. You can make it a totally unique variety all things considered. However, once more, we need to adhere to that standard of transformation enhancement and split testing. Furthermore, we can essentially have a three-way split test between three distinctive feature varieties and see which one plays out all that we could add another and have a four-way test. Does that sort of bode well, as long as it's only one component for each time, you can have however many varieties as you need.

Clearly you would prefer not to have such a large number of varieties since then you will not have as generous and measure of traffic going to every variety, and you will not have the option to trust and be sure of the outcomes so much. So, it's likely best to adhere to a few runs as much traffic as possible through those. Also, obviously it'll be parted similarly. So, on the off chance that you have three, it'll be, you know, 33, 33 and 33% going to each page. The following stage here is to sit and stand by and just let some traffic result in these present circumstances page until we have a generous sum that we can really be sure of you know, the outcomes, you know, since, in such a case that we have 10 individuals come through here and we saw that you know, this page has a 30% higher select in rates than the other page. It doesn't actually mean anything. It was a lovely little example bunch, 10 individuals. So, we need essentially something like, you know, 50 individuals to every variety, something around there before we begin making suppositions about the outcomes we see, and that is the thing that we will do straightaway. Alright. We will sit, delay until we have sufficient information. And afterward the following exercise we will investigate results.

Module Three

G ood. Welcome to module three. In this module, our master will show you breaking down the split outcomes. So, prepare to take a few notes and how about we directly bounce in.

Good. So, in this exercise, we will be going over some true instances of split test outcomes and how to kind of dissect them and how to manage those outcomes. So how about we view this one first. This is the page, the first page that we're taking a gander at. OK. Exceptionally essential page moderate feature logo at the top and the catch. What's more, it doesn't actually say anything regarding what it is. Indeed's, it's, this would be known as a visually impaired feature. OK. It's blinder than daze really. So, this was the first, and afterward it was parted tried several different variations. Also, we should view. So, variety, we should see here.

We should ensure I got that right. This is the first variety they're faulty in that line there. OK. That is the first. That bodes well. So, this is the first, and it has a tad of data about the item variety B probably was the visually impaired one. That's right. Also, variety C better believe it. Was somewhat like variety. A yet the primary feature was somewhat, somewhat more modest, however with more content in it. So, begin bringing in cash online with 200 or more free video exercises, begin bringing in cash online with our web showcasing foundation. So, this one has somewhat more detail in it. How about we examine what really was the victor. So, variety and as a large number of us likely might have speculated, did indeed, improve. It had the most elevated rate. There were 44.7% changes.

So out of 47 guests to that variety, 21 of them changed over, and that is a beautiful strong transformation rate. Also, there's a sorry contrast however, between that shockingly and the visually impaired one. While this one here, shockingly, I did the most noticeably awful 30%, 11.5% less. Presently, despite the fact that we have what most would concur is a sensible measure of traffic per variety to arrive at certain resolutions. This is really low. We would truly need to follow that and check whether variety see, which is basically the same as variety and is truth be told, that much more awful. What's more, does indeed play out that amount more terrible. It could be said that this one performs better on the grounds that it gets too unmistakable, there are the points of interest out in the fundamental feature 200 or more free video exercises while this one, a variety B performs well, since it's the contrary limit and visually impaired features do.

Truth be told, kind of electrifies individuals in some cases relying upon who you're focusing on, in case you're focusing on individuals in the MMO specialty to bring in cash online specialty, for instance, and they can't bring in any cash on the web and they see a visually impaired feature that in a real sense simply says, begin bringing in cash online the present moment, perhaps that is possibly that is the factor that made this one nearly as effective as the partner with the more definite feature. You know? So, the best way to know without a doubt is send more traffic to it. Nonetheless, in case you're running a live activity, you're not simply parted testing for entertainment only to recollect. You're, you're really maintaining a business with dollars and pennies. It's difficult. It's difficult to continue tossing cash into something that get-togethers much traffic appears to have a lower change rate. So as opposed to simply keep it going similarly, some may say it's smarter to simply leisurely dial it down so you can have a tad of traffic going there, which will be valuable for you know, inquiring up on that split test and checking whether the outcomes changed, suppose a month from now, yet you're not squandering an excessive amount of cash by losing that.

In the event that indeed it is dispassionately a fact that it performs less. Also, the way that you do that is simply changing the traffic parted. Presently, once more, contingent upon what programming you're using, this could conceivably be an alternative, or it may look somewhat changed, yet on Insta page, it's called traffic split and you can physically set the traffic split to anything you desire, totally anything you desire. So, assuming we need 15% going to variety, see, cause it's not doing extraordinary, however we need to keep collecting some more traffic and proof throughout the coming months. And afterward check once more. We can do that, but since these ones are making us the most elevated number of leads or the most noteworthy measure of cash at the present time, we need the vast majority of our traffic going there right now. Does that sort of bode well? Presently we should have one more glance at a comparable true model here and how about we see we'll stack up the varieties.

OK. So as should be obvious, there's a beautiful huge the contrast between these there's no in a dead heat, as on the past model, 79.4%, isn't crazy rendition rate for a lead page. How about we view what the thing that matters were. There's this, this, and this you'll see the feature is something very similar. The size of the case may change a smidgen. You know, the content is somewhat more extensive and that went with the features something very similar and these, the sub-feature is by and large something very similar. Also, the catch is by and large something similar. Presently this is the thing that's known as an extension page. Alright? So, this is a lead page where you catch a lead. In any case, what you're truly pitching is a video. Also, this case is on the off chance that our call the guest was, just shipped off a business video, a subsidiary offer, alright, yet variety C pardon me, variety.

A didn't perform awful using any and all means 38% is as yet a decent change rate, however it's the most reduced of these as somewhat odd, on the grounds that this is somewhat of a cool looking picture, yet I think a media or striking the earth appear to resound. This is an extraordinary looking picture, however perhaps it reverberated somewhat more straightforwardly being in the focal point of the screen and having part of spotlight on it. Part of differentiation there and the shadings, and it reverberated a great deal, or I should say it functioned admirably with the red words, historic earth, breaking, video changes, everything. You know, presently that was the general purpose of each of the three pictures. There's an image of pivotal. This one, that is disputable. Regardless of whether earth is really breaking, it appears as though, no doubt, it seems as though some kind of a planet is crashing into earth. Holler to those, what are they called?

Flawless Hebrew individuals out there. Be that as it may, for reasons unknown, this one was cosmically more well known.

Also, here's the arrangement when you're breaking down split test outcomes, not continually going to have an answer, you're not continually going to have a why. You know, you're not continually going to have the option to comprehend why this one and truly, a considerable lot of individuals who go to the page, will not have the option to disclose to you why. You know, there's simply mental marvel once in a while that are extremely challenging to make certain about in an unseat your work. In any case, except if you're an exploration researcher or something isn't really to stress and worry over the why. Indeed, you're keen on it's what and what for this situation is that you will get 80%, eight out of 10 individuals who you ship off this variety here will select in.

So, it's very utilized that variety more. Does that somewhat bode well? So, we would need, you know, we were looking at dialing it down and dialing it up. We would likely call this one. Great. OK. It's a ton of traffic, tremendous distinction in transformation, same traffic hotspot for this load of pages, you know, one traffic source to one greeting page with three varieties. That is to say, you should simply do this, you know, or even only 100% to variety B you know, you could wind down these ones. That is an unmistakable victor. So once more, here and there it will be somewhat strange. Try not to worry a lot about the Y albeit the Y can be helpful for future undertakings. So, in the event that you can and say it and can make certain about, by everything implies do as such, yet don't worry about something over the top. Cause you don't actually have to know the why you simply need to realize which one's performing best and put the entirety of your advertising endeavors into that one. Starting now and into the foreseeable future.

Don't miss out!

Visit the website below and you can sign up to receive emails whenever B. Vincent publishes a new book. There's no charge and no obligation.

https://books2read.com/r/B-A-QWUO-XEFRB

BOOKS 2 READ

Connecting independent readers to independent writers.

Also by B. Vincent

Affiliate Marketing
Affiliate Marketing
Affiliate Marketing

Standalone
Business Employee Discipline
Affiliate Recruiting
Business Layoffs & Firings
Business and Entrepreneur Guide
Business Remote Workforce
Career Transition
Project Management
Precision Targeting
Professional Development
Strategic Planning
Content Marketing
Imminent List Building
Getting Past GateKeepers
Banner Ads

Bookkeeping
Bridge Pages
Business Acquisition
Business Bogging
Marketing Automation
Better Meetings
Conversion Optimization
Creative Solutions
Employee Recruitment
Startup Capital
Employee Mentoring
Followership
Servant Leadership
Human Resources
Team Building
Freelancing
Funnel Building
Geo Targeting
Goal Setting
Immanent List Building
Lead Generation
Leadership Course
Leadership Transition
LinkedIn Ads
LinkedIn Marketing
Messenger Marketing
New Management
Newsfeed Ads
Search Ads
Online Learning
Sales Webinars

Side Hustles
Split Testing
Twitter Timeline Advertising

About the Publisher

Accepting manuscripts in the most categories. We love to help people get their words available to the world.

Revival Waves of Glory focus is to provide more options to be published. We do traditional paperbacks, hardcovers, audio books and ebooks all over the world. A traditional royalty-based publisher that offers self-publishing options, Revival Waves provides a very author friendly and transparent publishing process, with President Bill Vincent involved in the full process of your book. Send us your manuscript and we will contact you as soon as possible.

Contact: Bill Vincent at rwgpublishing@yahoo.com www.rwgpublishing.com